Princess Treasury

Princess Treasury

Three Classic Princess Stories

Snow White
Cinderella
Beauty and the Beast

Cartwheel
·B·O·O·K·S·®

SCHOLASTIC INC.

New York   Toronto   London   Auckland   Sydney
Mexico City   New Delhi   Hong Kong   Buenos Aires

For Barbara Milagros and Ayanna Josephine,
the fairest of them all
–M.A.T.

For Aunt Mary and Uncle Frank, with love always
–B.L.

Snow White (0-439-47152-4)
Text copyright © 2003 by Scholastic Inc.
Illustrations copyright © 2003 by Barbara Lanza.

Cinderella (0-439-47153-2)
Text copyright © 2004 by Scholastic Inc.
Illustrations copyright © 2004 by Barbara Lanza.

Beauty and the Beast (0-439-47151-6)
Text copyright © 2003 by Scholastic Inc.
Illustrations copyright © 2003 by Barbara Lanza.

10   9   8   7   6   5   4   3   2   1   5   6   7   8   9 / 0

Printed in China

ISBN: 0-439-74892-5
This edition first printing, September 2005

CONTENTS

Snow White

Cinderella

Beauty and the Beast

Snow White

by **Melissa A. Torres**
Illustrated by **Barbara Lanza**

Snow White was a princess.

She lived long ago.

Everyone but the queen loved Snow White.

The queen had a magic mirror.

"Mirror, mirror, here I stand.

Who is the fairest in the land?" the queen asked.

And the mirror said, "You are fair.

But Snow White is many times more fair."

The queen was mad!

She told a hunter to kill Snow White.

But the hunter would not kill her.

"Run away," he said. "And never come back."

Snow White ran and ran.

She was very tired.

Then she saw a little house.

Snow White peeked inside.

She saw seven little beds.

"I will take a nap," she said.

When Snow White awoke, she saw seven dwarfs.

The seven dwarfs were kind.

They let Snow White live in their little house.

The next day, the queen asked,
"Mirror, mirror, here I stand.
Who is the fairest in the land?"

The mirror said, "Snow White,
who lives with the dwarfs, is the fairest."

The queen was very mad!

She thought of an evil plan.

"I will give Snow White a poisoned apple.

She will die. Then I will be the fairest," she said.

The queen dressed up as an old woman.

Then she went to find Snow White.

When the seven dwarfs went to work,
she knocked on their door.
Knock! Knock! Knock!

Snow White looked out the window.

"I must not open the door to strangers," she said.

"That's all right," said the queen.

"I don't need to come in. But I want you to have this apple."

The apple looked so good!

Snow White took it.

After one bite, she fell to the floor!

The queen's plan worked!

She went home and asked,

"Mirror, mirror, here I stand.

Who is the fairest in the land?"

"You are the fairest," the mirror said.

"At last!" said the queen.

The dwarfs came home.

They found Snow White on the floor.

They tried to wake her.

But they could not.

The dwarfs placed Snow White in a glass coffin.

Then they put the coffin on a hilltop.

One day, a prince was walking in the forest.

He saw Snow White.

The prince fell in love with her.

The dwarfs let the prince
take Snow White to his castle.

Four boys carried the coffin.
One of them tripped on a rock,
and the coffin shook.

The bite of apple fell out of Snow White's mouth!
She sat up and opened her eyes.

She saw the prince and fell in love with him.

Snow White and the prince had a big wedding
and lived happily ever after.

The evil queen was sent far, far away.

And she never hurt anyone again!

To Princess Madison
–H.L.

In memory of my Cosentino and Lanza grandparents
–B.L.

Cinderella

by **Hara Lewis**
Illustrated by **Barbara Lanza**

There once was a beautiful girl
named Cinderella.

Cinderella had a mean stepmother
and two ugly stepsisters.
They made her cook and clean
and wear ragged clothes.

One day, the prince of the
land decided to give a ball.
Cinderella's stepsisters were invited.
But Cinderella was not.

The sisters tried on dresses to wear.

They made Cinderella fix their hair.

Cinderella, wouldn't you love to go to the ball?"
hey asked, laughing.

I wish I could go," Cinderella cried softly.

Soon it was the night of the ball.

The stepsisters rushed off to the palace.

Cinderella sat alone, crying.

Just then, her fairy godmother appeared.

"I will help you go to the ball, Cinderella."

The fairy godmother tapped
seven mice with her wand.
They turned into six fine horses
and a jolly coachman.

Then she waved her wand over a pumpkin.

It turned into a fancy coach.

She waved her wand once more.
Cinderella's torn dress
turned into a beautiful gown.
And pretty glass slippers
appeared on her feet.

"Now you must hurry,"
said the fairy godmother.
"The spell will end at midnight.
You must return home
before the clock strikes twelve!"

At the ball, the prince danced
only with Cinderella.
No one knew that Cinderella
was the beautiful princess.

The clock struck twelve.

It was midnight.

The spell was about to end!

Cinderella had forgotten about the time.

Cinderella ran from the palace.
One of her glass slippers
fell on the steps.

The prince ran after Cinderella.

He could not catch her.

He picked up the slipper and went back to the ball.

The prince wanted to find
the beautiful princess.
The next day, he took the glass slipper
with him into town.
He wanted every woman in the land to
try on the shoe.
"I will marry the one whose foot fits
this slipper," the prince said.

The prince reached Cinderella's house.
Her mean stepsisters pushed Cinderella aside.

They each tried on the slipper.

But it did not fit.

"May I try?" Cinderella asked.
Her stepsisters laughed at her.
But the prince placed the shoe
on her foot.

It fit perfectly!

Cinderella pulled the other slipper from her pocket.

She slid it on.

Her sisters were shocked.

Suddenly, her fairy godmother appeared.
She turned Cinderella's ragged dress
into a lovely gown.

"You are the one I danced with!"
said the prince to Cinderella.
"Will you marry me?" he asked.
"Yes," said Cinderella.

And Cinderella and the prince
lived happily ever after.

Beauty
and the
Beast

Adapted by **J. Elizabeth Mills**
Illustrated by **Barbara Lanza**

A rich man had three daughters.
The older daughters were selfish and mean.
But the youngest daughter was sweet and kind.

Her name was Beauty.
The older sisters did not like Beauty.

The father owned many ships.

One day, his ships were lost at sea.

The family became poor.

The older sisters didn't like being poor.

They would not do any work.

Beauty didn't like being poor, either.

But she cleaned the house and cooked.

Then the father heard that one ship was found.

"Hooray! We are rich again!" said the oldest sister.

The father set off to meet his ship.

"What would you like me to bring back to you?" he asked.

One daughter asked for dresses.

Another asked for jewels.

Beauty asked only for a rose.

But when he arrived,

the father saw the ship was ruined.

He had no money to buy dresses.

He had no money to buy jewels.

On his way home, the father passed a garden.
He picked a rose for Beauty.

Suddenly, he saw an ugly beast.

"That rose is mine!" said the Beast.

"Now you must die!"

"The rose is for my daughter," said the father.

"Then she may come to my castle in your place," said the Beast. "But she must want to stay."

The father returned home.

He gave Beauty the rose and told his story.

"This is Beauty's fault," her sisters said.

"I will live with the Beast," said Beauty.

Her father tried to stop her.

But the next morning, Beauty went to the castle.

"Do you want to stay here?"
the Beast asked.
"Yes," said Beauty.
"Will you marry me?" asked the Beast.
"No," said Beauty.

For three months Beauty stayed with the Beast.

He gave her beautiful dresses.

He gave her many books to read.

"The Beast is very kind," thought Beauty.

Each evening Beauty and the Beast ate together.

Each evening he asked her to marry him.

And each evening she said no.

One night, Beauty asked to see her family.

"You may go home," said the Beast.

"But you must return in eight days."

Beauty promised to return.

Then the Beast asked her to marry him again.

But again, Beauty said no.

The next day, Beauty went home.

Her father was happy to see her.

But her sisters saw her beautiful clothes.

And they were jealous.

Eight days passed.

Beauty's sisters begged her not to leave.

So Beauty agreed to stay.

"Perhaps the Beast will be angry and eat her!"

they said to each other.

On the tenth night, Beauty had a dream.

The Beast was dying.

Beauty awoke.

She felt scared and sad.

She had broken her promise.

Beauty rushed back to the Beast.

She found him in the garden.

"I'm sorry, Beast!" cried Beauty.

She kissed his ugly face.

"I know you have a good heart," she said.

"I will marry you."

Just then, there was a bright light.

A handsome prince stood before her.

"Where is the Beast?" she asked.

"I was the Beast," said the prince.

"But you saw my good heart instead of
my ugly face. You broke the spell."

And Beauty and the prince
lived happily ever after.

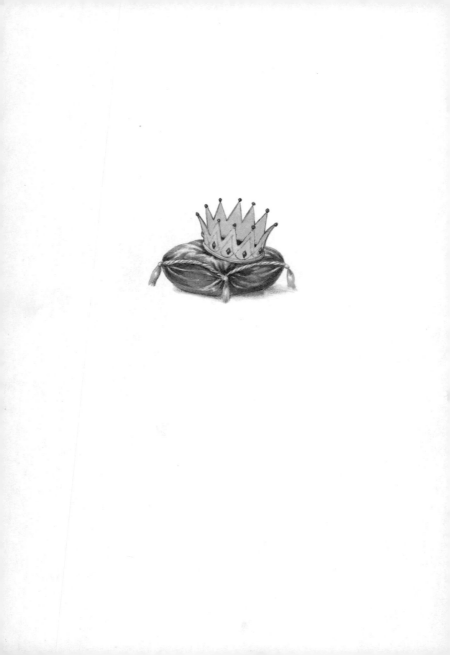